WORLD IN VIEW

INDIA

Nicholas Nugent

STECK-VAUGHN
L I B R A R Y

Austin, Texas

Library of Congress Cataloging-in-Publication Data

Nugent, Nicholas
    India / Nicholas Nugent.
    p.   cm.—(World in view)
    Includes index.
    Summary: A survey of the history, government, economy,
    natural resources, people, culture, and future prospects of
    India.
    ISBN 0-8114-2441-3
    1. India—Juvenile literature. [1. India.] I. Title.
II. Series.
DS407.N84   1991   90-25300
954—dc20   CIP AC

Cover: *Udaipur in Rajasthan*
Title Page: *The Ghats (Steps) on the Ganges at Varanasi*

Designed by Julian Holland Publishing Ltd
Picture research by Jennifer Johnson

Typeset by Multifacit Graphics, Keyport, NJ
Printed and bound in the United States
by Lake Book, Melrose Park, IL
1 2 3 4 5 6 7 8 9 0 LB 95 94 93 92 91

·**Photographic credits**
Cover: ZEFA/R. Everts
Title page: Jimmy Holmes/Himalayan Image, 5 Jimmy Holmes/Himalayan Image, 8 Jimmy
Holmes/Himalayan Image, 10 J. Allan Cash, 13 Gerald Cubitt/Bruce Coleman, 16 J. Allan
Cash, 20 Hutchison Library, 23 Popperfoto, 29 Robert Harding, 31 Popperfoto, 33 Christine
Pemberton/Hutchison Library, 37 Chris Caldicott/Himalayan Image, 39 Jimmy
Holmes/Himalayan Image, 41 Jimmy Holmes/Himalayan Image, 45 Brian Warriner/Robert
Harding, 47 Jimmy Holmes/Himalayan Image, 49 Hutchison Library, 50 Jimmy
Holmes/Himalayan Image, 52 Nancy Durrell McKenna/Hutchison Library, 53 Himalayan
Image, 55 Jimmy Holmes/Himalayan Image, 56 Robert Harding, 57 Jimmy
Holmes/Himalayan Image, 59 Jimmy Holmes/Himalayan Image, 61 Christine
Pemberton/Hutchison Library, 63 Jimmy Holmes/Himalayan Image, 64 Hutchison Library,
65 J. Allan Cash, 67 Maggie Murray/Format, 68 Maggie Murray/Format, 69 Jimmy
Holmes/Himalayan Image, 72 Maggie Murray/Format, 73 Sassoon/Robert Harding, 76
Jimmy Holmes/Himalayan Image, 77 Sassoon/Robert Harding, 78 Robert Harding, 79
Leslie Woodhead/Hutchison Library, 80 Christine Pemberton/Hutchison Library, 82 Jimmy
Holmes/Himalayan Image, 84 OXFAM, 86 Maurice Harvey/Hutchison Library, 87 J. Allan
Cash, 88 Chris Caldicott/Himalayan Image, 90 Robert Aberman/Hutchison Library, 92 J.
Allan Cash.

Contents

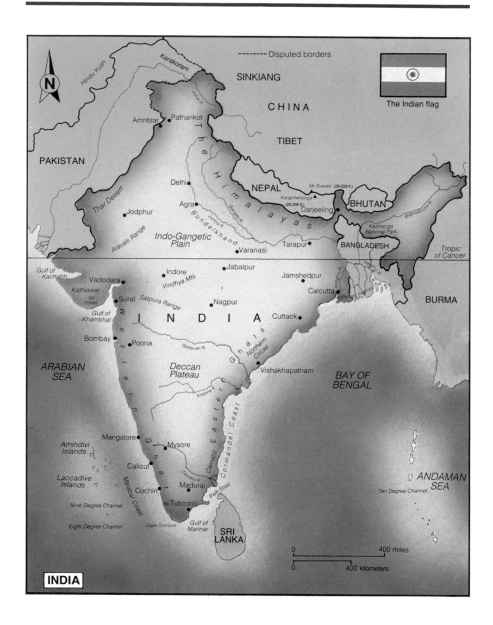

INDIA

1   Introducing India

India is a vast land that juts out of southern Asia into the Indian Ocean. The country stretches 1,500 miles (2,400 kilometers) from north to south, and the same distance from east to west. Its total land area of 1.27 million square miles (3.28 million square kilometers) makes it larger than the whole of the European Community and about a third the size of the United States. India is bordered on the east by Burma and Bangladesh. To the north, there are borders with Bhutan, Nepal, and China. To the west, India has a boundary with Pakistan. India and Pakistan are still in dispute over ownership of the northern territory of Kashmir.

The high peaks of the Himalayas are covered with snow throughout the year. No one lives on the highest mountains, but the lower slopes of the numerous river valleys provide land suitable for farming. During the summer these valleys are much cooler and more pleasant than the rest of India.

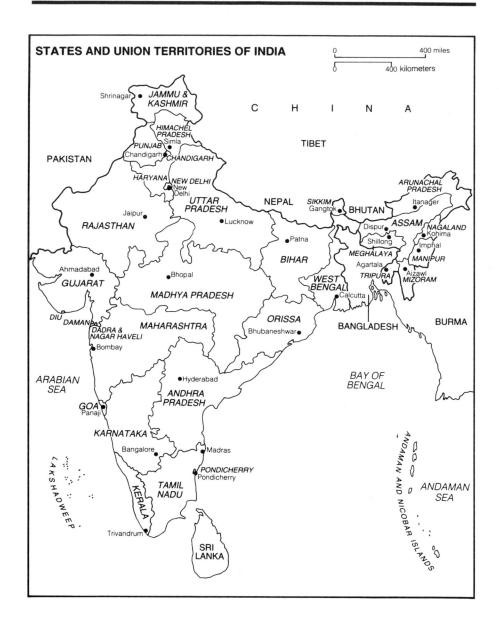

STATES AND UNION TERRITORIES OF INDIA

Indian Money
The unit of currency in India is the rupee. It is made up of 100 paisa. People use coins for purchases of up to one rupee, and paper money above that amount. A newspaper costs about one rupee. In the city, it costs between 20 and 50 rupees to have a good meal. It costs several hundred rupees to buy a buffalo.

Three great ranges of mountains, the Himalayas, the Karakoram, and the Hindu Kush, separate India and some of its neighbors from the Tibet and Sinkiang regions of China, and from Soviet Central Asia. Many of the world's highest mountains, including Mount Everest, are in these ranges. The area that this mountain barrier surrounds, which includes India, Pakistan, and Bangladesh, is often referred to as the Indian subcontinent. The subcontinent is a self-contained region and the mountains have helped to protect it from outside influences. Away from the mainland, India controls several small island groups. The Andaman and Nicobar islands are to

The Indian Flag and National Symbols
India's flag is made up of three horizontal bands of color; they are, top to bottom, saffron yellow, white, and green. The saffron yellow symbolizes the spiritual nature of India. Saffron is the color worn by *sadhus* or Hindu holy men. The white bar symbolizes peace, while green symbolizes wealth through agriculture. In the middle of the flag is a blue wheel, the Buddhist wheel of eternal life.

Large areas of India are covered with dense forest. Some of these forests have been turned into national parks. This small village is in the tropical forest of Madumalai National Park in the far south, very near the equator.

the east in the Bay of Bengal, between India and Indonesia. Off India's southwest coast, in the Arabian Sea, are the Lakshadweep islands. Not many people live on these islands, but they add to India's coastline, which in total is 3,530 miles (5,650 kilometers) long.

A land of contrasts

All of India lies to the north of the equator, and over half of the country lies within the Tropics.

The Tropics are the regions between the equator and the imaginary lines 23.5 degrees of latitude north and south of the equator. The country's position means that most of India has a hot, moist climate, but some of the high mountains in the north are cold enough to be covered by snow throughout the year. Some parts of the west of the country are desert and get little rainfall.

Most of India's land is used for agriculture, to feed the country's large population. About 20 percent is forested, though this percentage has declined in recent years because of the pressure to use land for growing food. In addition to farms and forests, India also has large cities and industrial areas. It is one of the world's top 20 industrialized nations; it builds its own fighter aircraft and has satellites in space.

India's population is around 800 million, and is increasing at the rate of 20 million each year. India has more people than all of the European countries added together, and more than twice as many people as live in North America. Every seventh person in the world is an Indian. Controlling the rate of population growth and feeding the people it already has are India's biggest problems. It is estimated that by the year 2000 India will have over one billion people.

Three broad regions
India can be divided into three main regions, based on their geographical features. The first region is known as the Himalayas, a name that means "the land of snow." These high mountains, which lie partly in neighboring countries, form an arc across the north of India.

The mountain ranges known as the Ghats or "steps" form the edges of the Deccan plateau, the remains of an ancient mountain system in central India. The stepped edges of the Western Ghats range for 1,000 miles (1,600 kilometers).

Few people live in this region. The three great rivers of north India, the Indus, the Ganges, and the Brahmaputra, rise in the Himalayas, their waters coming from the melting snows. These rivers flow down to India's second main region, the Indo-Gangetic plain, which extends from Punjab in the west to Bengal in the east. India's greatest concentration of people is in this region, which includes the states of Bihar, Uttar Pradesh, and Punjab. At the region's western end, along the border with Pakistan, is the Thar Desert, the driest area of India. At the region's eastern end, the Ganges and Brahmaputra rivers and their many tributaries combine to flow into the Bay of Bengal in the vast Ganges delta. This delta stretches from south of Calcutta into Bangladesh. Large areas of the delta are covered by jungle.

The Vindhya range of mountains stretches across India from coast to coast about halfway down the country. India's third main region, the Deccan plateau, lies to the south of these mountains. The plateau is around 3,300 feet (1,000 meters) above sea level. Between the plateau and the coast are steep slopes known as *ghats*. The Western Ghats border the Arabian Sea, and the Eastern Ghats overlook the Bay of Bengal. The Deccan plateau has its own river system. There is no melting snow to provide water for these rivers, so their size and flow vary enormously between seasons, depending on the amount of rain. The main rivers of the Deccan plateau are the Cauvery, Krishna, and Godavari.

The monsoons
The monsoon winds, which occur regularly at certain times of year, are important in determining the climate in India. Most areas expect one main period of rain, carried by the summer or southwestern monsoon. This begins in June or July and lasts until September. Seventy-five percent of the annual rainfall comes during this season and often leads to flooding. During the monsoon period, it usually rains at least once a day, often for a long time. When the monsoon starts, and how long it lasts, are the most important features of the weather in India, for they determine when and where crops can be grown. If the rains come late or end early there may be food shortages in some areas.

In September, the main monsoon ends and it gives way to the cold season in the north. However, some parts of the country, like the large southern state of Tamil Nadu, benefit from the northeastern monsoon at this time. The winds of this monsoon bring cooler, drier weather than the main monsoon. For most of the country, March or

April marks the start of the hot season, and dust storms are common. Temperatures can reach 117°F (47°C). The Himalayan region and other highland areas are cooler at this time of year and are popular as resorts where people who can afford it go to get away from the heat.

Wild animals and plants

India has some of the most spectacular and varied wild animals of any country. Among the rarer species are the lion, now few in number and confined to the Gir Forest in Gujarat, the tiger, the rhinoceros, and the Himalayan snow leopard. All these species are protected by the government, which has set up more than 200 national parks and wildlife sanctuaries to preserve the habitat in which the animals live. Other rare animals include panthers, cheetahs, and a single species of panda. Elephants, camels, and buffaloes are relatively common because they have been

Major Indian Wildlife Sanctuaries
- Gir Forest, Gujarat, home of Indian lion
- Sundarbans Swamps, West Bengal, home of crocodiles and the Royal Bengal tiger
- Kaziranga National Park, Assam, home of the one-horned rhinoceros
- Corbett National Park, Uttar Pradesh, home of the tiger and many other species, and a favorite center for people on wildlife-viewing safaris
- Dachigam National Park, Kashmir, home of the Kashmir stag or hangul
- Ranthambhor National Park, Rajasthan, another tiger sanctuary

Elephants are widely used in India for carrying large loads or doing heavy work such as hauling timber. These elephants are carrying fodder in a reserve for tigers, which are now one of India's endangered species.

trained to carry men and goods. Monkeys, crocodiles, lizards, and snakes are also common. One of India's snakes, the king cobra, can grow up to 13 feet (four meters) long, and is the biggest of all poisonous animals. There are said to be about 1,400 species of bird in India. One of the more common birds is the mynah. The peacock India's national bird, is also plentiful in some regions.

India also has a very varied collection of plant life, mainly due to the wide range of elevations and climates. There are all types of forests, and many varieties of palm tree on the plains. In the northeast of the country savannah grass and bamboo are found. In the Himalayas, laurels, maples, and birch can be found side by side with conifers and rhododendrons. Ebony, teak, and sandalwood grow in the south.

13

2 History of a Nation

There is definite evidence that people were living in the Indian subcontinent nearly 5,000 years ago. That means Indian civilization is as old as some of the other early civilizations, like that of the Pharaohs of Egypt, builders of the pyramids. The earliest signs of life in the subcontinent have been found on the banks of the Indus River, which flows through the northern region known as the Punjab, or land of the five rivers. Nowadays Punjab is divided between modern India and its neighbor, Pakistan. Excavations on the banks of the Indus at Harappa and Mohen-jo-daro, both in present-day Pakistan, reveal a highly developed system of town planning and drainage. Streets were laid out in an orderly manner, and there are remains of public buildings like baths, granaries, and assembly halls. Houses, made out of kiln-fired bricks not unlike the bricks used today, were built around courtyards.

Ancient inscriptions and pictures on pottery and other items from both Harappa and Mohen-jo-daro suggest the early inhabitants of the Indus Valley were wealthy farming people. Similar inscriptions have been found at the site of another early civilization at Mesopotamia (Iraq) indicating that there was trade between these two areas. Historians, who have tried to interpret the inscriptions, cannot agree about where the people who lived in the Indus Valley came from. One theory is that the people were of south Indian, or Dravidian, origin. Others believe that they may have migrated overland from Europe.

There is disagreement, too, as to what brought the civilization in the Indus Valley to an end. A popular theory is that the civilization was destroyed by invaders from Europe who are known to have settled in northern India around 3,500 years ago. Another theory postulates that the weather was responsible. Possibly the river flooded, destroying the cities, or perhaps the weather pattern changed. Today Mohen-jo-daro is so dry that hardly anything grows there.

New empires and religions

In around 1500 B.C., settlers from Europe known as the Aryans arrived in northern India. Their arrival was an important event; they were eventually to give India its main religion of Hinduism. Like the earlier peoples, the Aryans also settled at first in Punjab, attracted by the richness of the soil which even today makes this one of India's best farming areas. Later the Aryans spread eastward into the Ganges Valley. Quite a lot is known about how the Aryans lived because of their writings, in particular the great epic poem, the *Rig Veda*, and the two famous legends, the *Mahabharata* and the *Ramayana*. The era of the Aryan settlers is known as the Vedic Age because the *Rig Veda* became the centerpiece of their form of worship. Vedism, or the Vedic religion, is considered to be the earliest form of what is now known as Hinduism.

The Vedic religion led to the establishment of a rigid social structure in which people were classified into groups, or castes, according to their jobs or social status. It was into this age, shortly before Jesus Christ was born in another part of the

Over 2,000 years ago the Indian Emperor, Ashoka, made Buddhism the state religion of India. He erected a great pillar at Sarnath to commemorate the place where Buddha preached his first sermon. The lions from the top of the pillar have become India's national symbol. They are displayed in the Sarnath Museum, Uttar Pradesh.

world, that two great social reformers arrived on the scene in northern India. Both were to reject the caste structure of the Vedic religion and start their own religions. Vardhamana Mahavira founded the religion known as Jainism, in which meditation and respect for the sacredness of life are important aspects. Buddhism was founded by Siddhartha Gautama, who took the name Buddha, meaning Enlightened One, after receiving a revelation that made him understand what he was to do. Buddhism later spread throughout Southeast Asia. Around the year 260 B.C. one of India's most famous rulers, the Emperor Ashoka, adopted Buddhism and made it India's main religion. Ashoka succeeded in extending his kingdom, the Mauryan empire, from the Hindu Kush mountains in the west of the Indian subcontinent to Assam in the east, and as far south as Mysore in Karnataka. Ashoka united many small states under his rule, and he is credited with having united India. For that reason, Ashoka's lion remains the national symbol of India today. After Ashoka's death in 232 B.C., the Mauryan empire went into decline, giving way eventually to the Gupta empire, a prosperous and stable period in which religion was less important.

Muslim rule in India

About a thousand years after Ashoka's death, in the eighth century, another great religion arrived in India. Islam had been founded about 100 years earlier on the Arabian peninsula by a saintly man named Mohammed, who wrote down the word of God, or Allah, in the book known as the Holy Koran. The followers of the Islamic religion became known as Muslims. At first, Islam only spread to the far northwest of the Indian subcontinent. Later Punjab came under the control of the Muslim ruler of Gazni in Afghanistan. By the end of the twelfth century, Hindu princes throughout north India were paying tribute to the Afghan ruler, QutbudDin Aybek, who had set himself up as king of Delhi.

The next invasion of India came 200 years later. Another Muslim ruler, Timur, swept down from the central Asian city of Samarkand with 90,000 men and horses to attempt to overthrow the king of Delhi. Timur walked with a limp, and was known as Timur the lame, or Tamerlane. Despite his handicap, he conquered much of Asia, from Persia to India. Tamerlane's capture of Delhi was to establish the Mughal dynasty, when his descendant, Babur, became emperor. Mughal rule, however, was challenged, and the throne at Delhi was recaptured for a while by the Afghans before Babur's son, Humayun, re-established the dynasty. Humayun's son, Akbar, strengthened Mughal rule over most of India during a reign of nearly 50 years from 1556 to 1605. During the period when Akbar's son, Jahangir, was on the throne, Britain made its first contacts with the rulers of India. In 1615, King James I sent an ambassador, Sir James Roe, to pay his respects at the Mughal court. After Jahangir died the throne passed to his son, Shah Jahan, who built the magnificent Taj Mahal in the city of Agra in Uttar Pradesh.

Shah Jahan was succeeded by his son, Aurangzeb, who again had to resist challenges to his rule both within the empire and beyond it. The Afghans attacked again, but were driven back, while in Punjab, Aurangzeb was challenged by the followers of another new religion. Guru Nanak (1469–1538) had tried to work out a way in which Hinduism and Islam could be combined. He created the religion of Sikhism, which is founded on some beliefs from both of the original faiths.

Toward the end of the seventeenth century, Guru Gobind Singh, the most famous of the Sikh gurus or teachers, made the region of Punjab into a state under his control, thus challenging the rule of the Mughals from nearby Delhi. This set an example of breaking away from central rule that others were to follow. Some of the powerful Hindu rulers of the north, like the Rajputs and the Marathas, as well as local Muslim chiefs, like the rulers of Hyderabad and Oudh in the south, reinstated their independence from Mughal rule. Aurangzeb's death in 1707 marks the beginning of the decline of the Mughal empire, though Mughal rulers remained on the throne in Delhi for another 150 years.

European domination

The British were not the first Europeans to arrive in India. That claim is made by the Portuguese who, in 1510, captured the southwestern region of Goa and set up a number of trading posts. They were followed by the Dutch and the French and finally by the British, who were anxious to follow their European neighbors to this rich new source of spices. The first British trading post was set up in 1612 at Surat, to the north of Bombay, by a private company, the British East India Company. This company had been formed to bring about trade with India. Later the Company established a settlement at the southern city of Madras, and then another at the port city of Calcutta, which was to become the center of British business and political influence in India. For 150 years, the British presence in India was that of a commercial company trying to make money for its

The hills of Rajasthan surround the beautiful marble palace of Udaipur, which appears to float on Lake Pichola. The palace, which is now a hotel, was completed over 200 years ago as a summer home for the reigning maharaja, whose family declared itself independent of the Mughal rule.

shareholders through trade, and the British government was not directly involved.

Before establishing their rule or *raj*, the British first had to fight their European rivals, notably the French traders. Madras twice changed hands, but eventually the British, under Robert Clive, forced the French to retreat to Pondicherry. Pondicherry, which is surrounded by present-day Tamil Nadu, remained under French control for 200 years. Clive also captured French settlements near Calcutta and defeated the army of the Nawab of Bengal at the Battle of Plassey in 1757. Clive fought on behalf of the British East India Company, but his successes on the battlefield against both European and Indian rivals laid the basis for the British government's direct involvement in ruling India in the 1800s.

After the Battle of Plassey, Warren Hastings became the first Governor General of the area then known as British India, centered on the province of Bengal. Hastings refused to pay tribute to the Mughals, who, though weakened, remained on the throne in Delhi until 1857. As a result of Hastings's actions, there followed a series of military encounters in which the British strengthened their position. The last of four wars fought for control of the southern state of Mysore ended in 1799 with the defeat and death of Tipu Sultan, the southern ruler most determined to fight off British advances. In the west, the Marathas were eventually defeated in 1818, while the Sikhs in the north held out for a little longer. The British finally captured Punjab in 1848 after a series of Anglo-Sikh wars. Several weaker states were then captured in quick succession.

British rule suffered a shock in 1857 from the event known in Britain as the Indian Mutiny and in India as the First War of Independence. The British East India Company had set up an army, with Indian soldiers filling the lower ranks. However, the Indians resented the attitude of the British officials of the Company, who ignored the traditions and customs of their Indian staff and soldiers. Even the court system introduced by the British apparently terrorized those who came before it. It was run by British judges who were ignorant both of the language and the customs of the people on whom they enforced their will. There was, by this time, a strong anti-British feeling among Indians. Some historians believe that Britain's policy of excluding Indian leaders from positions of power in the Company, the army, and the administration was the major cause of the revolt.

The British response, after putting down the mutiny, was to transfer control of India from the East India Company to the government in London. After 1857, governors appointed by the Company gave way to viceroys appointed by the government. The word viceroy means "in place of the king." There was a change of policy too, with the British less determined to decrease or destroy the power of local rulers. From this time on, the British were content to leave in power the local princely rulers, the sultans, the maharajahs, and the nizams, and to serve merely as their "advisers" rather than as foreign master. Even so, the British viceroys of India had more power than the king or queen of England, and over many more people. In 1877, Queen Victoria was proclaimed Empress of India in addition to her British titles. In 1911, her son, King George V, visited India to attend the Delhi *durbar*, the ceremony that marked the formal transfer of the British seat of power from Calcutta to the Mughal capital, Delhi.

The independence movement
In 1885, nearly 30 years after the British government assumed control of India, the Indian National Congress, or Congress party, was formed. Twenty years later, the Muslim League was founded. Both organizations had as their main purpose the ending of British rule in India. When Indian troops were sent to Europe to help Britain in World War I in 1914, both organizations passed resolutions demanding that Indians be

Gandhi, dressed here only in the Indian loin cloth or dhoti, earned the nickname "Mahatma," which means "Great Soul," for his campaign of nonviolence and noncooperation in seeking independence for India. He also campaigned for the development of Indian crafts and to improve the status of the poorest people. He was never a member of the government but worked closely with Nehru, who became prime minister, in negotiations with the British.

allowed to rule themselves. Indians did not see why people from so far away should be in charge of their country, which was so much bigger than Britain. This resentment against the British was increased because the British treated the Indians as inferiors. However, the British did not want to leave such a valuable colonial possession. Trade with India had made a lot of people in Britain wealthy, and had helped Britain's Industrial Revolution. Raw materials for industry, such as cotton and timber, as well as spices and tea, were brought from India as well as from Britain's other colonies.

At about the time of World War I there arrived on the scene a British-trained lawyer who played

a vital role in the drive toward independence. Mohandas Karamchand Gandhi, later to be called "Mahatma" Gandhi, or simply "Gandhiji," inspired the Congress party to pursue its demand for independence by refusing to cooperate with British officials. He suggested that people should disobey the British authorities, but should not take part in violent protest. Although violence did break out, it is India's proud claim to have won independence largely through peaceful means. One of the most violent incidents during the struggle for independence occurred in the city of Amritsar in Punjab. In 1919, a British general rashly ordered his troops to open fire on an unarmed crowd, killing several hundred people. The brutal massacre at Amritsar caused great anger and resentment among the Indians and spurred on the independence movement.

Talks between the Congress party and the British authorities continued, but the British seemed reluctant to leave India. Eventually, in 1930, Gandhi began a mass civil disobedience movement with a symbolic gesture. He marched to the seashore in his native state of Gujarat and deliberately broke the law by collecting salt and refusing to pay the government the tax that it imposed on salt collecting. Gandhi and 100,000 supporters were arrested.

When World War II broke out in Europe and Indian soldiers were again pressed into service, demands for independence grew. The Congress party demanded that the British "quit India" immediately. After World War II, a weakened Britain realized that independence for India was inevitable. The disobedience campaign had made it increasingly difficult to rule the country.

The British viceroy, Earl Mountbatten, was authorized by London to make arrangements for independence. He found, though, that the Muslim League was now determined to have a separate Muslim state. Though the British and the Congress party wanted India to remain one country, the Muslims, who did not want to be dominated by India's Hindu majority, were determined to have their own country. So, when the British finally left, large parts of the northwest and the northeast of the country were separated from India to form the new nation of Pakistan. The division of the subcontinent into India and Pakistan, known as Partition, was accompanied by massive bloodshed, as Hindus and Muslims migrating to their new homelands started killing each other. Both new countries came into existence as independent nations at midnight on August 14, 1947. Jawaharlal Nehru, who became the first prime minister of India, called this moment "the redemption of a tryst with destiny." By this he meant that this moment of freedom was inevitable, and that it was the Indian people's right to rule themselves.

Independent India

Nehru was India's prime minister for the first 17 years of independence, a period which saw wars with both Pakistan and China over disputed territory. However, one of the first crises during his leadership came a few months after independence, when Mahatma Gandhi, who was regarded as Father of the Nation, was shot dead by a Hindu extremist. The assassin resented

Pakistan and India

Pakistan separated from India at the time of independence in 1947. Muslims were worried that Hindus, who outnumbered them by about two to one, would dominate the independent state of India, so they insisted on having their own state of Pakistan. Almost everyone in Pakistan is a Muslim. There are also plenty of Muslims in India as well as followers of other minority religions, such as Sikhism, Jainism, and Christianity.

Immediately after the division of British-ruled India into India and Pakistan, the two new countries went to war with each other over who should control the northern state of Kashmir. The ruler of Kashmir was a Hindu and wanted to be part of India, but most of the people who lived there were Muslims. War broke out a second time in 1965, but still the problem of who should control Kashmir was not settled. Kashmir continues to be split between India and Pakistan along what is known as the cease-fire line.

A third war between India and Pakistan took place in 1971, but for different reasons. India stepped in to help the Bengali people of East Pakistan, who felt they were getting a bad deal from the country's rulers in West Pakistan. The eastern people's language, Bengali, was not given the same importance as the Pakistani national language of Urdu, and the eastern wing of the country was underdeveloped compared with West Pakistan. The short war ended with East Pakistan becoming the independent nation of Bangladesh. So the land of India, which was ruled by the Mughals and then the British, is now divided into the three separate nations of India, Pakistan, and Bangladesh.

the way Gandhi, who was also a Hindu, preached tolerance toward followers of other religions, and had opposed the creation of a separate Muslim nation.

One of Nehru's first tasks after becoming prime minister was to persuade the princes who ruled around 460 independent states that they should give up their rights and accept the authority of the government in Delhi. The princes agreed to this in return for a salary or privy purse from the central government. The princely states were merged into the pattern of larger states, or administrative units, into which India is now divided. Having taken control of British-ruled India, the government also set itself the task of recovering the only part of the country still ruled by foreigners. In 1961, the Portuguese were driven out of the southern state of Goa, which they had ruled for 450 years.

After Jawaharlal Nehru died in 1964, having held office as prime minister for 17 years, Lal Bahadur Shastri became prime minister for a brief period. When he died in 1966, power passed to Nehru's daughter, Indira Gandhi, who led the country for most of the next 18 years. Her time as prime minister was not without problems, and in 1975 Mrs. Gandhi felt threatened by a popular movement against her rule. She claimed that the country was slipping into chaos, and imposed a state of emergency, which resulted in the stopping of civil rights, including that of free speech. Newspapers were censored by government officials. The state of emergency lasted from 1975 to 1977, when Mrs. Gandhi called new elections. The people showed that they were not pleased about this period of harsh rule by voting the Congress party out of power for the first time and electing a non-Congress government.

This non-Congress government collapsed after two and a half years and Mrs. Gandhi returned as prime minister. She then ruled firmly until she was assassinated in 1984 by Sikh members of her bodyguard. They were angry at the way she had sent the Indian army into the holiest shrine in the Sikh religion, the Golden Temple at Amritsar, to try to capture gunmen hiding there. Many soldiers and gunmen died in that incident, known as Operation Blue Star.

Under Mrs. Gandhi, India had become a considerable power in the world. It is sometimes called a regional superpower because it is so much bigger than most of its neighbors. After Mrs. Gandhi's assassination, she was succeeded by her son, Rajiv. Some people claimed that Indian politics had become a family affair. Rajiv Gandhi, a former airline pilot with only limited political experience, did not find it at all easy to follow in his mother's footsteps. Ruling a country the size of India is difficult even for an experienced politician. Rajiv Gandhi has tried to carry on his mother's role in international affairs. He has traveled widely and involved himself in the affairs of the British Commonwealth and of the United Nations. He has also taken part in talks aimed at ending apartheid in South Africa and bringing about international disarmament.

3 Government and States

The spacious Raj Path or Government Road in the capital city of New Delhi leads toward the domed Rashtrapati Bhavan, the residence of the president of India. The British moved the capital from Calcutta in 1911 and built a new city with very grand public buildings to display their power and influence.

India's system of government has borrowed a great deal from the British. It is a parliamentary system with two chambers or houses of parliament. The people of India directly elect representatives to the Lok Sabha, the Council of the People. The upper house, the Rajya Sabha or Council of the States, is made up of representatives elected by the assemblies of each state. There are 25 states, each with its own elected assembly or ruling body. There are also

seven union territories, Delhi among them, which are ruled by governors appointed by the central government. The Indian constitution defines which powers are held by central government and which by the state assemblies. Many decisions are made by the states.

President, prime minister, and parliament
Like the United States India has an elected president. However, he or she is elected by members of parliament and the state assemblies instead of the people. The president of India does not have as much power as the president of the United States, but is more like the British Queen, having a mainly symbolic role. However, the president does have the authority to appoint the prime minister, and to replace him or her if the prime minister no longer has the support of a majority in parliament. The president also signs into law acts passed by parliament.

The president of India lives in the country's capital, New Delhi, in a rather imposing palace, Rashtrapati Bhavan. It was built during the time of British rule for the viceroy to live in. Nearby is the round parliament building, which was also built by the British. Proceedings in parliament can get very noisy and members speak in different languages. Fortunately, there is an interpreting service on headphones.

The most important person in India is the prime minister. The job of prime minister goes to the person whose party wins the most seats in parliament at the general election. General elections for seats in the Lok Sabha have to be held every five years.

Political parties

Nehru, Mrs. Gandhi, and Rajiv Gandhi all led the Congress party, India's oldest political party. This party has ruled India almost continuously since independence from Britain in 1947. There are plenty of other parties, but none is as well organized as Congress throughout India. Some, like the Communist parties, are powerful in certain areas, and control some state governments. Other parties only operate in one state. They are known as regional parties and tend to be dominated by one or more powerful local politicians. Regional parties have tried to work with national parties to defeat Congress at the elections. However, the opposition parties have often failed because of rivalry between party leaders as to who should have the top jobs.

Indira Gandhi speaks to an agitated Sikh petitioner during one of the regular audiences she held in the garden of her residence. Two weeks after this photograph was taken, Mrs. Gandhi was killed by two Sikh members of her own security force.

> **Some of the Main Political Parties**
> - Congress—This party has split several times since it was first formed. The main party is now called Congress-Indira, or Congress-I for short, after Mrs. Gandhi, who led it for many years.
> - Janata Dal, or People's Party
> - Bharatiya Janata Party
> - Communist Party of India
> - Communist Party Marxist
> - Akali Dal—a regional party of Punjab
> - Telugu Desam—a regional party of Andhra Pradesh
> - Dravida Munnetra Kazhakam—a regional party of Tamil Nadu

Elections

More than 400 million people in India are eligible to vote. This electorate is larger than that of any other nation. When Rajiv Gandhi decided to reduce the voting age from 21 to 18, it meant that nearly 50 million extra people joined the electorate, more than four times the number in that age range in the U.S. Organizing elections is therefore a complicated and expensive business, because so many polling places have to be set up. Nearly a half million are needed for a general election. Voting takes place over three or more days because of the difficulty of collecting ballot boxes from remote regions. Large sums of money are spent by the parties on persuading the people to vote for their candidates, who conduct campaigns much like politicians in Western democracies. Many people in the villages cannot read or write, so the voter puts an "X" on the

Elections in the State of Kerala are taken very seriously, as elsewhere in India. There is usually an enormous turnout of voters and enthusiastic campaigning by the various political parties.

ballot by an election symbol familiar to everyone, perhaps a hand or a bicycle, of the candidate of his or her choice. Each person has one vote and no one is excluded because he or she comes from a low caste. Each voter may select only one candidate. The general election will determine which of the 5,000 or more candidates are chosen to occupy the 545 seats in the Lok Sabha, and as a

33

consequence which of the political parties is able to form a government and provide a prime minister to rule the country.

The states, the army, and the legal system

Some of India's states have more people than many independent nations. Uttar Pradesh, with a population of around 125 million people, would, if independent, be the world's eighth largest nation, having about the same population as Japan. So the chief minister of a state like Uttar Pradesh has a great deal of power. A state chief minister has a cabinet of ministers to assist in running the state. Both the state and the central government have an administrative service which carries out the orders of the elected politicians and runs, among other things, the schools, the hospitals, and the railroads. Matters like foreign affairs and defense, though, are the responsibility of the central government rather than state governments.

If for any reason the government in a state collapses, the central government can take over the running of that state until it is possible to hold state elections again. This has happened in Punjab, for example, because of the violence there. The army may also be sent to settle any problems. India has a very large army, the fourth largest in the world, as well as an air force and a navy. Traditionally the armed forces have not interfered in the running of the country, as they have done in some other countries. They take their orders from the politicians, who decide whether the police and authorities need the help of the army to deal with any local disturbances.

Besides providing a model for the Indian parliament and army, the British left India an elaborate legal system. Judges in national and state courts uphold the laws that have been passed by parliament. No politician is above the law and many, including Mrs. Gandhi, have found their actions questioned and even ruled illegal in the courts of law. Any citizen of this huge country has the right to take a dispute to court, though unfortunately the judges, like the politicians, are not always as free from corruption as they should be.

4 A Variety of People

One in every seven people in the world lives in India. Only China has more people. With around 800 million people, it is inevitable that there is a huge variety of races, religions, languages, and castes in India. An Indian can tell a great deal about a fellow Indian by looking at him or her. For example, the style of clothing, such as the way a woman ties her sari, reveals a great deal about a person. The colored marks a woman puts on her face may reveal her caste and whether or not she is married, while a man may wear a turban, a sacred thread around his wrist or neck, or a bangle on his arm, all of which may be symbols of his caste or religion. A further clue to identity comes from the language or dialect a person uses; names also reveal something about a person's place of origin, religion, and caste. What he or she eats, in particular whether the person is a vegetarian, will give a further clue as to caste.

Historically, the major division of the Indian people is between the Aryans and the Dravidians, or the migrants who arrived in north India and the original peoples of south India. This division is evident in racial characteristics. Generally, southern Indians are darker skinned than northern Indians. People of other racial types are found in India in smaller numbers and are generally concentrated in the remoter regions of the country, like the Andaman and Nicobar islands, and the areas to the north and east of Bangladesh. These people are often described as tribespeople.

These Hindu women, from the State of Orissa on the east coast, are dressed in beautiful saris made of cotton or silk. Their skin is dark and they are wearing jeweled pins in their noses as is the tradition in many parts of India. The red marks on their foreheads are called bindi, and are a symbol of happiness. Married women also have a mark on their forehead.

Language

Most people in India think of themselves in terms of their language group, considering themselves to be, for example, a Bengali, a Tamil, or a Punjabi as much as an Indian. The Indian constitution lists 15 major languages, known as scheduled languages. Apart from Sanskrit, a language of scholarship that is not in everyday use, the others are all widely used. The list on page 38 shows that around 200 million people speak Hindi or one of its dialects, such as Rajasthani or Bihari. Four other languages are spoken by more than 50 million people in India. Bengali, which is spoken in Bangladesh as well as India, is the sixth most widely spoken language in the world.

India's Scheduled Languages
Hindi: the national language, widely spoken throughout northern India by around 200 million people, including speakers of dialects
Bengali: 55 million speakers in West Bengal, plus 100 million in Bangladesh
Telugu: 55 million speakers in Andhra Pradesh
Marathi: 53 million speakers in and around Maharashtra
Tamil: 50 million speakers in Tamil Nadu plus a small number in neighboring Sri Lanka
Urdu: 46 million speakers in various parts of India. Urdu is also the national language of Pakistan.
Punjabi: spoken by 20 million inhabitants of Punjab state, and many more in Pakistan
Gujarati: 33 million speakers in Gujarat. Gujarat is also an important business language.
Kannada: 28 million speakers in Karnataka
Malayalam: the language of the state of Kerala, spoken by 26 million
Oriya: spoken by 24 million inhabitants of Orissa
Assamese: the language of Assam, with fewer than 10 million speakers
Sindhi: the language of the Pakistani province of Sind, but with speakers in India too
Kashmiri: the language of Jammu and Kashmir
Sanskrit: a language of scholarship with very few native speakers

Though India has many different languages, the situation is less complicated than it appears, because many of the scheduled languages are related to each other. For example, speakers of the

Members of this family from the Himalayan region of Arunachal Pradesh have the pale skin and Mongoloid features of many of the peoples of the Himalayas. Their ancestors probably came from central China and Tibet.

"northern" languages of Hindi, Punjabi, Bengali, Gujarati, and Marathi can generally understand each other; there are similarities, too, between Tamil, Malayalam, Telugu, and Kannada. Besides the main languages, there are around 90 nonscheduled languages. Some of these have a few million speakers, others only a few thousand. Figures from surveys show, though, that nine out of every ten Indians speak one of the scheduled languages, even if it is not their first language. The variety of languages, and particularly the marked differences between the southern and northern languages, helps explain why India has retained English as a link language, used widely in government and business. On Indian railroads, for example, timetables, tickets, and

39

notices are all displayed in English, a language with which the ticket collector and the ticket sales agent will be familiar as well.

The Indians had intended to do away with English in favor of Hindi as the national language 15 years after independence. This plan, which should have come into effect in 1962, was abandoned in the face of opposition from southern Indians, who believed that making Hindi the national language would give an unfair advantage to northern Indians in getting government jobs. Instead, English, which is understood by many, has been retained. Each state is allowed to determine the language in which its state administration operates. Official government policy is to encourage the learning of up to three languages, namely a person's mother tongue, Hindi, and English.

Religion and caste
Religion is another way in which Indians are divided. Since religion plays a very important part in everyday life, religious differences are more important than they would be in North America or Europe. The majority of Indians, or around 83 percent, are Hindus, with Muslims, totaling 11 percent, making up the largest minority. Other religious communities are the Christians, the Sikhs, the Buddhists, the Jains, the Parsis, and the Jews. Religion in India is considered in more detail in the next chapter.

Hindus, and some non-Hindus too, are divided into groups called castes. Hindus are born into their caste just as they are born into their religion. There are four main castes. These are,

Sikhs are forbidden by the rules of their religion to cut their hair. The men wear their hair wound up in a turban that can be made from up to 55 feet (17 meters) of cloth. In Rajasthan, different groups wear different-colored turbans. The light skin and narrow faces of these Rajasthani men show that their ancestors were the Aryan people, from whom many European peoples are also descended.

from highest to lowest castes; the Brahmins or priests; the Kshatriyas or warriors; the Vaisyas, who are traders or farmers; and the Sudras, who carry out unskilled or craft work. Within these four main castes there are numerous sub-castes or regional variants. The caste may indicate a trade. Just as the Brahmin is the priest, the Chamar is the cobbler or shoe mender, and members of the Dhobi caste wash clothes. In some cases the caste indicates the place of origin. For example, Brahmins from southern India may belong to the Ayyangar, Ayyar, or Nambudiri caste, while the Jats, found in north and northwest India, are a farming caste, who also have a reputation as fine soldiers. The Marathas are a land-owning caste from west India, while the Nayars are the warrior caste of the southern state of Kerala.

41

The Rajputs are a princely caste, originally from the western state of Rajasthan, who are famous for their interest in and support of the arts. They developed the practice of adding "Singh," meaning lion, to their names, a practice later adopted by Sikhs. Non-Indians often mistakenly believe that someone called Singh must be a Sikh, but this is not necessarily so.

At the bottom of the social scale are the castes of landless laborers and fisherfolk. Today these people are given special protection by the law because of their poverty. Some of India's tribal groups, or people from minority racial groups, are similarly protected. More than 100 million Indians belong to what are called scheduled castes and another 50 million come from scheduled tribes. These are castes and tribes that are included in a schedule or list attached to the Indian constitution because they are deprived or disadvantaged in some way. Mahatma Gandhi, the leader of India's independence movement, called the members of such castes "Harijans," or "Children of God," rather than "untouchable," the term by which they had been known in the past. Although government policy is to break down caste barriers, old customs die slowly and many high-caste Hindus will still not share a table with, or eat food prepared by, someone from a low caste. The caste system is deeply ingrained in Indian society, much as class distinctions are elsewhere.

5   Religion in India

Though India is a secular state, meaning that no one religion is regarded as a state religion, religion does hold an important place in people's lives. That is hardly surprising in a country that has given birth to two of the world's major religions, Buddhism and Hinduism, as well as lesser ones like Jainism and Sikhism, and has absorbed many other religions.

The Hindu majority

A majority of Indians, around 83 percent (or more than 650 million people), are Hindus. Their religion had its origin with the coming of the Aryans to the Indian subcontinent more than 3,500 years ago. The religion of the Aryans was known as Vedism, the name coming from their religious texts or Vedas. The Vedas are the oldest religious texts in the world and are based on stories older still. Hinduism has undergone changes from the Vedism of the Aryans. However, Hinduism today is more a way of life than a religion. At its heart lies the belief that a person's soul may be born again after death, in another body. This is called reincarnation.

Hindus believe in a variety of gods. People vary in the importance they give to the different deities, or godlike figures. For example, some worship the god Brahma, the creator, others worship Vishnu, the preserver, while others pay their respects to Shiva, the destroyer of evil. All over India there are ornate temples dedicated to these gods, and to others. Some people say that

Major Hindu Gods and Goddesses

Brahma, the creator. Depicted with four heads and four arms, holding a spoon, a vessel of holy water, a chain of holy beads, and a book of the Vedas. Brahma is frequently shown seated on a lotus, the plant from which he is believed to have been born. Usually he is accompanied by his wife, Saraswati, who is represented mounted on a peacock or sitting on a lotus flower, holding in her hands another lotus flower and a stringed musical instrument called a vina. Saraswati is the goddess of divine knowledge and of understanding.

Vishnu, the preserver. Vishnu is represented in many forms, including those of Rama, the conquering hero whose deeds are celebrated in the epic Ramayana legend, Krishna, the king's son who became a cow-herd, or Buddha, the Hindu warrior who founded his own religion. Vishnu is often shown reclining on a snake while his wife, Lakshmi, meditates at his feet. Lakshmi is the goddess of beauty, grace, divine benevolence, and riches.

Shiva, the destroyer of evil. Depicted with four or eight arms, symbolizing his universal power. The arms hold a mace or battle-axe, the conch shell used to call people to prayer, a small drum symbolizing the saying of the alphabet, and a sacred wheel representing the cycle of rebirth. Shiva rides on a bull, Nandi, and is accompanied by Parvati, goddess of beauty and love. Among their children are Ganesh, the elephant-headed god, and Kali, the goddess of Calcutta, who is usually shown riding on a tiger. Kali is also the goddess of death.

These statues of Hindu gods show Ganesh, the elephant-headed god, and Hanuman. Ganesh is a popular god because he is believed to help with the success of any project that is undertaken. Hanuman, the monkey god, is one of the main characters in the Ramayana legend. There are many temples to Hanuman in India.

Hinduism has only one all-powerful god and that Brahma, Vishnu, and Shiva are different ways of representing that one god.

Hindu beliefs and life styles

When non-Hindus say that you can be a Hindu and believe anything, they are not being disrespectful, for the variety of beliefs within the faith is enormous. Toleration of rival beliefs is an important feature of Hinduism. The ways in which Hindus practice their faith vary enormously, too. Some regularly attend temples to worship, while others prefer to worship at the altar that can be found in every Hindu home. Holy days are important, but there are many of them, with different days being observed in different regions or by followers of the different gods. In Calcutta, Durga Puja is important, being associated with the city's own goddess, Kali. In Kerala, Onam is an important festival associated with Bali, one of the representations of Vishnu, while Tamils attach much importance to Pongal. One thing that tends to unite Hindus, though, is the pilgrimage, or *mela*, which brings people from many parts of India together. Popular places for such gatherings are on the banks of the Ganges River. Hindus consider the Ganges itself to be a goddess, and bathing in its waters a sacred act, bringing forgiveness for sins.

There are variations too in life style, though broad practices are similar. The caste system is still an important feature of Hindu life and many Hindus do not like to mix with people of a lower caste. Most Hindu men take only one wife, though the religion permits more than one. It is common for a bride's family to pay a dowry by giving money, land, or goods to the bridegroom's family. Many Hindus, especially those from the higher castes, such as the Brahmins, are vegetarian, and do not eat meat or fish. No Hindus will eat beef, believing the cow to be a sacred animal. All Hindus attach enormous importance to cleanliness, and washing is an important part of their daily ritual. Hindus tend to be superstitious. They take a great deal of notice of omens, or signs of the future, and consult astrologers before choosing a date for an important event, like a marriage. Horoscopes of marriage partners are generally matched, too. After death, it is customary for Hindus to be cremated, unlike Muslims, who favor burial. The practice of suttee, where a widow commits suicide by throwing herself into the flames of her husband's funeral pyre, is illegal today, although it continues occasionally in certain areas.

India's other religions

Muslims, the people who follow the Islamic religion, are India's second largest religious community. They number around 90 million people and are dispersed widely throughout the country. In Jammu and Kashmir they are in a majority, but everywhere else they are outnumbered by Hindus. The Mughal empire helped Islam establish itself as a major religion in India. Muslims are not grouped into castes, as the Hindus are, but are divided into categories known as sects. Most Indian Muslims belong to one of the majority Sunni sects, but there are some who follow the minority Shia sect.

The minarets of the Jama Masjid mosque in Old Delhi soar above the main building. Mullahs, or Muslim teachers, call the Muslim faithful to prayer from the minarets. There are numerous mosques all over India for the 90 million Muslims who are summoned to pray five times a day.

The Muslims' holy book, the Koran, requires that Muslims pray five times a day. They are required by the Koranic teachings to try to make a pilgrimage to the Muslim holy city of Mecca in Saudi Arabia once in their lifetime. Muslims do not eat pork, which is considered unclean. As with Hindus, there is a ritual about the Muslim day, of which washing and praying are important parts. Muslims and Hindus often live side by side, so a lack of sensitivity by followers of one religion about aspects of the other may lead to clashes. This often happens when one faith is celebrating a holy day.

Sikhism, Jainism, and Buddhism, the other religions that started in India, have all in different ways broken away from Hinduism. Buddha rejected the caste structure of Hinduism. The religion he founded, about 2,500 years ago, after achieving enlightenment while meditating under a fig tree, emphasizes nonviolence, the doing of good deeds, meditation, and escape from suffering. The founder of Jainism also rejected the Hindu system of castes. Jainism goes even further than Buddhism in teaching respect for all forms of life. Devout Jains can be seen wearing veils over their mouths to prevent them from accidentally swallowing, and therefore killing, insects.

Sikhs, who generally can be recognized by the brightly colored turbans worn by the men, are well known for their fighting skills as well as for their talents as drivers, mechanics, and traders. Their faith, while in part a rejection of Hinduism, remains similar to Hinduism, but has also borrowed ideas from Islam. As with Islam, Sikhs respect a sacred book, the *Guru Granth Sahib*. In

The Golden Temple at Amritsar in the far northwest of India is the holiest shrine of the Sikh religion. The temple is built on an island in a small lake called the ''Pool of Immortality.''

recent years Sikhs have clashed with the central Indian government, which they feel has become dominated by Hindus. The Sikhs want greater recognition for their faith. Some have also demanded that the Sikh homeland of Punjab break away from the country of India to become an independent state.

49

6   The Indian Family

Most of the people in India live in the country. Whole families work on the land, where much of the work is still done without machines. These Kashmiris are harvesting rice by hand.

More than 75 percent of Indians live in villages in the countryside rather than in cities. They live in small houses, usually made of mud. It is common for several generations to live together in an extended family. If the house is small, the women will sleep in one room, and the men in another. Since very few houses have electricity, people tend to get up when the sun rises in the morning, and go to bed when the sun sets. They earn their livelihood by tending the crops in their own fields or by working in someone else's fields in return for a daily wage. Unless there is factory work or another source of employment nearby, both the husband and wife work in the fields. At harvest or

planting time, the whole family may have to help. A well-off family may also tend its own vegetable garden, and perhaps keep chickens or goats, or even a buffalo.

Food

Farming families store rice or wheat in their own homes after the harvest. For their other needs, they go to a market to buy food to add to the produce grown at home. In rural areas, there may be a market only once a week, so it is necessary to buy food supplies to last a whole week. Most food in India is bought fresh, and bottled or canned food is uncommon. Curry powder, for example, does not come from a jar. It is mixed from raw spices as part of the preparation of a meal. Refrigerators are rare in rural areas, and keeping foods fresh can be a problem, especially in the hot season. In the cities, where refrigerators are now quite common, but the electricity supply is unreliable, people still prefer to go to a market almost every day so that their food is fresh.

The family will probably have one main meal in the day, and one or two smaller meals. The cooking is done by the women, and they generally use an open stove. Plenty of spices are used in cooking. Meat may not be eaten every day, and is not eaten at all in vegetarian households. Hindus never eat beef, and neither Hindus nor Muslims eat pork, which they consider to be unclean. Chicken, goat, and buffalo meats are readily available. Near the sea, fish provides a source of protein. Lentils provide a nutritious and cheap vegetable dish. Other common vegetables are potatoes, cauliflower,

Families who work in the cities are often wealthier than those who live in the country. They have electricity and piped water. However, Indians still live in larger family groups, like this family of father, sons, and their wives, who share an apartment in Calcutta.

onions, and okra, a long green vegetable also known as "lady's fingers." There is a wide variety of fruit available, including mango, guava, orange, banana, and melon, as well as the large, red, thirst-quenching watermelon. Eggs are eaten, but milk and cheese are not readily available. *Ghee*, or clear butter, is used as a cooking oil. In rural areas water may have to be carried some distance from a well, unless a tube well or pump has been installed in the village. Finding water can be a big problem, especially in the dry season when rivers dry up. For fuel, it is common to use animal dung that has been dried in the sun, wood, or oil.

In rural areas, collecting water is one of the major tasks of the day. Sometimes people have to walk several miles to collect water, especially in the dry season. The water is frequently dirty and many people get diseases and die from contaminated water.

City life

In the cities, the contrast between rich and poor is more obvious than in rural areas. Rich families may live in large homes with expensive furniture and decorations. They may have one or more cars, and probably several servants. It is not unusual for even a moderately well-off family to employ servants. Work as servants provides income for a poorer family, so well-off people consider it to be a social duty to provide employment. A rich family may employ a cook, a nanny to look after the children, a *dhobi* or washer, a sweeper, a nightwatchman, and a driver. The servants themselves may be provided with accommodations by the family for which they work, or they may live elsewhere, possibly in one of the low-cost housing projects that are being built around India's main cities.

The poorest people in the cities are likely to live in slums, in shelters constructed from cardboard or corrugated iron sheets. The slums are unlikely to have suitable toilet or washing facilities. Bombay in particular has a very large slum area, while in the overcrowded city of Calcutta a great many people live their whole lives on the city's streets. Beggars are common, and they provide a sharp contrast to those people who live in the city's wealthy suburbs.

Marriage

Marriages in India are almost always arranged. It is the responsibility of parents to seek out a suitable partner for their son or daughter. A suitable partner would be one from the same religion and caste, and educated to a similar level. Parents of a particularly attractive girl would expect to find a partner who was likely to earn a good and steady income, one who has a job in government service, for example, or who is training to become a lawyer or accountant. The parents also have to consider the bride price, or dowry. This is the money, land, or property that the groom's family expects to receive from the bride's family as part of the marriage deal. Marriage-making is a big business in India. In the cities, parents often advertise in newspapers for a partner for their son or daughter. Sometimes, the advertisement will say "caste no bar" or "dowry not required."

The bridegroom in this marriage procession is given a place of honor by riding on a horse. In India, most marriages are arranged by the parents and it is quite usual for the bride and groom never to have seen each other. Both bride and groom keep their faces covered during part of the ceremony.

Finding a marriage partner for a daughter is probably the biggest, and almost certainly the most expensive, responsibility facing parents. It will be followed by an elaborate marriage ceremony and feast that may last more than a day. Nearly everyone gets married, often when the couple is still in their teens. The government has been trying to encourage later marriage as a way of helping to reduce the number of children being born. After marriage a bride will go to live with her husband's family. The couple may not have met each other before the marriage ceremony. Sometimes a bride will go home "on leave" to her parents for a while to help her adjust to her new situation. It can be quite a difficult experience for a young bride, especially if her new husband's family lives far from her own. However, most arranged marriages seem to work well. Indians, after all, grow up expecting to have a partner chosen for them. Today, it is increasingly common for people in the cities to choose their own marriage partner, although arranged marriages are still more usual.

Entertainment

Watching movies is a favorite pastime in India. There is a massive movie industry, mainly in Bombay and Madras, which produces about 700 movies a year. Actors and actresses, like Tina Minum who is shown here, are national heroes.

Television is becoming widespread in India, but is still rare in village homes. A well-off village might have one TV set, which villagers cluster around to watch. However, television as a form of entertainment is of limited value if the electricity supply cannot be relied upon. Movies are a more usual and very popular form of entertainment. India makes more movies than any other country,

Cricket is India's national sport and it is played both at the international level, where it draws enormous crowds, and in villages and towns. Bombay Park has dozens of cricket fields (pitches) that are regularly crowded with players. Here a field is being made smooth and even.

but then Indians watch more movies than most other people. In villages without theaters, makeshift projection arrangements are set up, often outdoors. Indian movies tend to follow a pattern, almost always involving a lot of singing. Moreover, in some areas there is a tradition of dancing, such as the famous Kathakali dancing of Kerala. Dance performances may also be held to mark a religious festival.

In the cities, television in homes is more common. City people may have a choice of different theaters, and these are always well attended. There may also be concerts of classical Indian music on traditional instruments like the sitar and tabla. These performances sometimes last all night. In the larger cities, there may be

57

drama, either in a local language or in English. Such cities may also be visited by foreign musicians, rock stars, or dance troupes. Teenagers in the cities enjoy an evening out as much as teenagers in the western world do.

The larger cities also have sporting facilities. Indians have a fondness for cricket, a game they came to love during the time they were ruled by the British. Nearly all Indians will follow closely the progress of their national team at home or abroad. Another popular team game is field hockey, in which India is one of the world leaders. Although the country is near some of the world's highest peaks, mountaineering has a rather limited appeal in India. However, there is the Himalayan Mountaineering Institute in Darjeeling in northern West Bengal, and Indians have been to the summit of many of the highest Himalayan peaks. Most sports, including mountaineering, are popular in the army.

7 Agriculture, Forestry, and Fisheries

Even in large cities like Varanasi, cows are allowed to roam freely in the street. They are considered to be sacred animals by the Hindus, so they are left alone, although they often lie in the middle of the road and cause traffic jams.

It is estimated that a quarter of the world's cows live in India. Cows are sacred to Hindus, so they are not kept for their meat. The quantity of milk they produce is low because they only get a limited amount of food. Yet cows are important in India for two main reasons. The first is to provide a means of transporting goods and plowing fields. Secondly, the manure or dung the cows produce is collected and used both as a cooking fuel in the home and as a fertilizer for crops. Water buffaloes are also common in India. Unlike cows, they are a source of meat, and also produce some milk. Bull buffaloes are used in the fields, too.

If there were no cows, the cost of doing the plowing and transportation jobs that they carry out would be enormous. It would be necessary, too, to find an alternative source of household fuel. Of course, it would be nice if the cows gave a plentiful supply of milk as well, but for that to happen they would have to be given better food, instead of being left to scavenge for scraps. Cows are allowed to wander freely in the streets of India's cities; this means that they perform another valuable function as cleaners, eating any vegetable matter, like banana skins or orange peel, that has been dropped. Indians also keep other scavenging animals that need little upkeep, like chickens and goats, and India probably has more of these than any other country.

Growing enough

Cows and buffaloes are important in the fields because India is mainly an agricultural country. It has to be to feed its enormous population. Until a few years ago, India was never certain from one year to the next whether it could produce enough food to meet its people's needs, especially if the monsoon rains did not come or arrived late, or if flooding washed crops away. It is still not possible to predict what the weather will do, but careful planning has ensured that even in a bad year no one starves. A government agency buys up extra grain in years when there is a surplus, and this is put into reserve in case there are shortages. This also has the effect of keeping prices stable, because if prices in the market begin to rise, food reserves are released onto the market to bring down prices.

India produces well over 60 million tons of rice a year. Cows and buffaloes are used to help with work on the land, especially plowing the wet soil needed for rice growing. These two cows have been decorated with red-painted horns and a pattern of dots to celebrate Holi, *the festival of colors.*

Around half of the land area of India is used for growing wheat, rice, or other staples, like pulses (legumes), which are used to prepare the popular vegetable dish, *dahl*. There are two main crop seasons, linked to the two monsoons. The *kharif* season begins in May and depends on the southwest monsoon. The crop is harvested around October. The *rabi* season starts in mid-October, and depends on the northeast monsoon to produce a crop that is ready for harvesting in April. Rainfall is the most important factor in the success or failure of the crop, though the amount of extra water or irrigation the crops are given is also important. Well-irrigated areas can expect to harvest two crops each year.

Rice is the basic or staple food in most of the country, but wheat is popular in the northwest, where it is used to make types of Indian bread known as *chappatis, nan,* and *parathas.* During the 1960s, great advances were made in wheat production with the introduction of high-yielding types of wheat. This resulted in what is known as the "Green Revolution" in the northern Indian farming states of Punjab and Haryana. Attempts to introduce these high-yielding varieties in other areas have not been so successful, partly because so much farmland has yet to benefit from irrigation. Another factor that determines the amount of grain that can be grown is the use of fertilizers. India is a major producer of fertilizers, but many farmers have low yields because they cannot afford the fertilizers.

Other crops
Farming in India is not just a means of feeding the people, but also a way of bringing in money. Around 70 percent of the population lives off the land. In addition to growing grain and vegetables to feed themselves, farmers also grow what are called cash crops. Cash crops include vegetables, fruits and spices that can be sold at the market. Some of these are sold abroad as well. For example, India is the world's largest producer of tea and peanuts or groundnuts. Tea is grown in Darjeeling in the north of West Bengal. India is also one of the leading producers of sugarcane, jute (which is used in making of sacks and carpets), and various types of vegetable oil. Many different spices are found in India and some of them are sold abroad.

Water supply is a constant problem in India, where there is either too much or too little. India has about 38 percent of its cultivated land under irrigation. Only China has more irrigated land. This simple irrigation system in Gujarat allows the banks of the ditches to be easily broken at certain points to flood the fields. In other areas massive dams have been built across rivers and there are plans to harness the monsoon flood waters.

Indians are particularly skilled in making use of many parts of a plant. The parts not used for human food may be fed to animals. Even the coconut plant has many uses. It provides coconut flesh and coconut oil for cooking, as well as fiber for the carpet industry, while the hard outer shell of the fruit is used to make handicrafts.

Forests

About 20 percent of India's land area is covered by forest. In the north, on the cold slopes of the Himalayas, subalpine conifers grow, while in the Sunderbans of West Bengal, where the Ganges flows into the sea, there is tropical rain forest. Today, government regulations ensure that forests are not cut down unless they are replaced. The government would like to increase the area

In many regions, forests have been cut down and arid areas are being created. The government has been encouraging the planting of a variety of trees. Fruit trees, like this mango tree, are popular because they provide a source of fruit for the family and a product that can be sold in the market or even exported.

covered by forest, to protect wildlife and prevent land erosion, when rainwater washes away the soil. In 1950, the government introduced an annual tree planting festival, Vanamahotsava, to make people aware of the importance of trees. Many people use the occasion to plant fruit trees like mangoes or figs, which help to feed their family. Many varieties of fruit grow in India.

Forests are an important source of firewood. They also produce bamboo and soft pine wood, as well as prized hardwoods like teak. Other products that come from trees include gum and resins such as turpentine. Leaves, in particular, have many uses, and those of over 20,000 different types of plants are used in traditional medicine. The leaf of the kendu plant is dried and wrapped to make the *bidi*, a small cigarette that Indians are fond of smoking. Other leaves are used instead of plates, especially in south India where it is considered unclean to eat off a plate that someone else has used; a leaf-plate can be thrown away after it is used. Leaves are also used to make cups, or for wrapping fruit and other goods in the markets or bazaars.

Fisheries

With 3,530 miles (5,650 kilometers) of coastline, as well as many big rivers, fishing is a valuable source of food as well as an important activity in India. More than a million people earn their living by catching and processing fish. For the people of the coastal states of West Bengal, Orissa, Tamil Nadu, Kerala, and Maharashtra, fish is a staple food. The state where fishing is most important is Kerala, because it has inland waterways as well as a long coastline. In Tamil Nadu pearl fishing, or extracting pearls from inside oyster shells, takes place. Other by-products of fisheries are isinglass, which is used in making jelly and glue, fish meal, on which chickens are fed, and fish manure, which is used as a fertilizer.

These fishermen are working on the Ganges near Patna. Most of the fish eaten in India is caught in the sea, but large rivers like the Ganges are a major source of freshwater fish. Many fishermen have joined one of the 7,152 fishing cooperatives in order to make fishing more profitable.

8 Industry, Trade, and Energy

In terms of the amount of goods made in its factories, India comes about fourteenth in a list of industrialized nations. However, because most of the goods made in the factories are used in India and not sold abroad, India is not generally thought of as an industrialized nation. Yet India has the technical skills to produce all its own steel. There are factories to build cars, and many "high-tech" industries making watches, television sets, video cassette recorders, computers, and other sophisticated electronic goods. India even manufactures its own fighter aircraft.

State-run and private industries
India's recent governments have believed that the country's main industries should be owned by all the people and be run on their behalf by the government. In many other areas of industry, however, private citizens are free to set up their own businesses. Many have become very rich by doing so. Activities that are state monopolies, meaning that private business may not take part, include the railroads and other transportation industries, weapons production, and the generation of most forms of energy including nuclear power. The coal-mining and steel-making, aluminum-smelting, engineering, shipbuilding, fertilizer producing, paper-making, and banking industries are mostly run by the government.

A variety of industries

India has some of the largest deposits or reserves of iron ore in the world. It also has large quantities of coal. Iron and coal are the main raw materials for making steel, and these reserves have enabled India to develop a large steel industry. The industry was centered originally at Jamshedpur in Bihar. Other steel smelters are in West Bengal, Orissa, Madhya Pradesh, and Karnataka. India is in the process of making use of its reserves of aluminum and copper ores in the hope of reducing its imports of these metals, and eventually producing enough to export. India also has chromium, manganese, and nickel.

More Indian people work in the textile industry than in any other industry. Though most cloth is

The textile industry provides work for millions of Indians in growing cotton, spinning, weaving, printing, and making the cloth into garments. The workers in this Bombay factory are printing cloth by the silk-screening method. The design is cut out of a waxed paper sheet and colored ink is pushed through the areas where the protective wax has been cut away. Each color is printed separately.

processed in large mills and weaving factories, a great deal of cloth is also produced at home or in what are called cottage industries. During the struggle for independence, Mahatma Gandhi encouraged Indians to avoid paying government taxes by spinning and weaving cotton and other fibers in their own homes. Homespun cloth, called *khadi*, remains very popular, and perhaps demonstrates most clearly the underlying Indian desire to be self-sufficient and not dependent on goods produced in factories or brought from overseas. Nowadays, most states sponsor and encourage home and small-scale industries, of which textiles are the most important. The goods that are not needed by the people who make them are sold through emporia, or large shops, where the selling prices are set by each state government.

Mahatma Gandhi encouraged the use of home industries, particularly spinning, to develop the economic independence of India. Different methods of spinning are used in different areas, and there are millions of homes where spinning cloth provides extra income.

One of the most important new areas for Indian industry is electronics. For some time electrical goods, like radios, televisions, and video cassette recorders, have been made in India. Now the move is toward "high-tech" products like calculators and computers. Bangalore in Karnataka in the south has traditionally been the center of specialist electronic and other

69

engineering, but such industries are now becoming established in Punjab, too. Other important industries are food processing and the manufacture of chemicals and medicines. After the textile industry, the largest area of employment is probably the construction industry, with at least three million full-time workers, and probably the same number employed on a part-time seasonal basis.

Foreign trade

One of the biggest obstacles preventing India from becoming a major industrial power is that it does not sell abroad enough of the goods it makes. This is due to two main reasons. The first is that India cannot produce enough goods to meet the needs of its own huge population. There is always a waiting list to buy a motor scooter or car, for example. The second reason is that, even if there are surplus goods, their poor quality may mean that nobody abroad wants to buy them. This applies as much to surplus food, as it does to goods made in factories, like bicycles. Indians have no choice but to buy Indian-made goods, because there are no foreign goods in the stores. Indian industry is protected by the government from the competition that foreign goods would provide, and therefore it has no need to improve the quality of its own goods. While India can take pride in producing most of what the country's people need for themselves, most Indian goods are of inferior quality and thus not attractive to foreign buyers.

India has generally had more success in what is known as import substitution, that is, reducing its needs for imports. Food grains and oil have been the major successes. India now produces and refines almost all its own oil needs, thanks largely to the reserves in the Bombay High oil-field off the west coast. It is possible that, within a few years, India will be able to export both crude and refined oil.

India's main imports are machinery and other engineering goods that it is unable to produce for itself. Curiously, though, India's single biggest import is uncut diamonds. These are cut and polished, particularly in Bombay, and then many of the finished stones are exported. Among India's major exports are tea, coffee, spices, cotton clothing, jute, leather goods, and handicrafts, as well as chemicals and engineering goods usually bound for neighboring countries. An increasingly important source of income is foreign tourists. Around a million people visit India each year to see the many sights. The government is eager to encourage visitors to come to India, and for this reason considers the improvement of its airlines, railroads, and hotels to be very important.

Energy
India's major sources of energy are manpower and animal power, since so much transportation depends on these. Farm fields are usually plowed by cattle or water buffalo. Even today a tractor in India is still a relatively rare sight. Another important energy source, whose value can only be guessed at, is animal dung or manure, which is dried and then burned in village homes to provide heat for cooking. Dung can also be used

to produce biogas, or methane. These animal energy sources are important because if they were not there the country's energy costs would be much higher.

Other major energy sources are coal and lignite, a form of coal. India has large reserves of both. Most of the gas and kerosene needed to run vehicles is refined from oil produced within the country. The main production areas are off the west coast and in Assam, but reserves have also been found in Tamil Nadu, Andhra Pradesh, and Gujarat. A pipeline is under construction to carry the natural gas that has been found in the Bombay High field, so that it can be used in industry or as a household fuel. Electricity is made from coal, water power, and nuclear fuels.

India has large deposits of iron ore that are used in the steel industry. This has developed into a large industry, producing nearly 30 million tons of steel as pig-iron, steel ingots, and finished steel. However, the further development of the industry is lagging due to lack of power and coal to fire the furnaces.

One of India's major problems is a lack of energy. Programs are being developed to work out ways of conserving energy and using resources that are easily available. This simple solar oven uses only the heat of the sun to bake food.

India is one of only nine countries in the world that has the ability to design, construct, and operate a nuclear power station. The first nuclear power station was commissioned at Tarapur in Maharashtra in 1969. The three stations now in operation generate less than three percent of India's electricity. Most villages still do not have electricity, but providing electricity for rural areas is a government priority.

9 Transportation and Communications

It is often said that the greatest gift the British left India is the railroad. India's is, indeed, a remarkable railroad system, the fourth largest in the world. It stretches the length and breadth of the country, more than 37,000 miles (60,000 kilometers) in all. It is used heavily for carrying both goods and passengers. Around 3.5 billion passenger journeys are made in the country each year. Very few people in India own their own cars, so public transportation is the main means of travel; the bicycle and buffalo cart are the usual forms of transportation within and around the villages. Buses are widely used as well, but trains are preferred by most people for all except short journeys. Train travel is also comparatively inexpensive.

Transportation Statistics
Railroad track 38,430 miles (61,850 km)
National highways 19,490 miles (31,360 km)
Other surfaced roads 330,000 miles (530,000 km)
Number of cars in use about 1 million
Number of motor scooters about 2.5 million
Number of bicycles about 30 million
Navigable waterways 8,700 miles (14,000 km)
Number of passenger aircraft 85
Number of merchant shipping vessels 407

Traveling by train

Between large cities, such as Madras and Bombay, there are likely to be several express trains running each day. Indian trains provide a choice of several classes of travel. The lowest-class cars are very basic, with hard wooden seats. Travel in air-conditioned class cars is comparatively comfortable, and the air-conditioning keeps out the dust that gets into everything in the non air-conditioned classes. For longer journeys, such as the one between Madras and Bombay, which takes a day and a night, it is also possible to reserve a sleeping berth. Both vegetarian and non-vegetarian food is served on board the trains, and during the journey young boys and girls wander through the car offering cold drinks, nuts, and other snacks for sale.

Even long-distance trains will stop several times during the journey. Most stops are for ten minutes or more, so passengers have time to step down onto the platform to drink a cup of tea, buy some fruit or perhaps a newspaper or novel from the station newsstand. The train may also stop for a long time between stations at signals, and there may be hold-ups during the monsoon season if the line has been washed away, or if villagers have cut a gap in the embankment to allow water to flow away. In order to enjoy traveling on Indian trains, passengers have to learn to be very patient. It helps that everyone tends to be friendly and quick to make conversation. Railroad stations are quite a center of activity, with many people waiting to catch a train or to meet someone disembarking. Many stations have a restaurant, and rooms where passengers can sleep.

Railroads are a very important method of transportation in India, carrying 3.5 billion passengers a year. The narrow-gauge railroad that climbs up the steep Himalayan foothills to Darjeeling is an amazing feat of engineering. Darjeeling is a popular place to visit because it has spectacular views over the mountains.

In the hilly areas, trains often travel on narrow-gauge tracks. The track may wind backward and forward as it crawls up the mountainside. At one point, the famous Darjeeling railroad even loops back over itself in a figure-eight pattern. At another place, it runs down the main street of a town. Two engines are needed to haul this train up the steepest gradients.

Indian trains are always crowded. On the slow suburban trains, many people try to avoid buying a ticket by climbing onto the roof to travel. This is difficult if they are carrying a lot of luggage with them. Very little of the railroad system is electrified, but diesel locomotives have largely replaced the old steam engines.

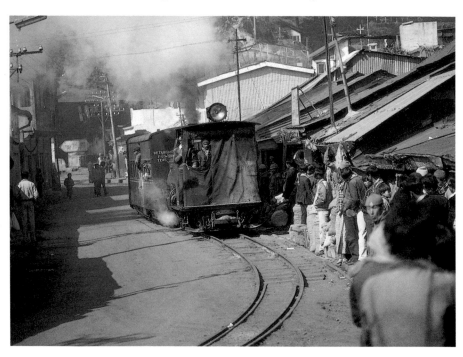

This busy waterway is in Alleppey, in the beautiful state of Kerala. The backwaters of Kerala are one of the main ways of travel through this important spice-producing area. The British influence can be seen in the uncharacteristic design of the church tower rising behind the houses.

Roads and waterways

The Indian government has been accused of neglecting roads in favor of railroads. Still, there are more than 18,500 miles (30,000 kilometers) of national highways, the main roadways that connect state capitals, ports, and other important cities. Buses hurtle along, with the drivers blasting the horn to warn people to get out of the way. Accidents are common, and it is not unusual to see buses or trucks that have gone off the road because the brakes failed or because the driver had to swerve to avoid another vehicle. Different tax rates are charged by each state, and trucks carrying freight may be delayed for a long time as they cross from one state to another. Officials often inspect the loads to see if any state taxes need to be paid.

In two states, Kerala and West Bengal, inland water transportation continues to be important. It

77

Many of India's rivers are too wide for bridges, so ferries operate to carry both passengers and vehicles from one bank to the other!

is one of the cheapest forms of transportation, both for people and for freight. People travel from northern to southern Kerala along what are known as the backwaters, stopping occasionally for refreshments at a waterside restaurant. At many of these restaurants the food is served on a banana leaf, and coffee is drunk out of an unfired mug which, for hygienic reasons, will be broken after use. It eliminates washing up!

Air travel and shipping

India has an elaborate air travel system connecting all major cities, many of them by several flights a day. The international airline, Air India, connects Delhi, Bombay, Calcutta, and Madras with other Asian countries, as well as

Television reaches over 60 percent of the population, although with the development of satellite broadcasting this should expand rapidly. Not everyone can afford a television set and it is quite usual for a whole village to share one or, in towns, for people to watch television outside a shop for several hours.

North America and Europe. These days it is possible to fly nonstop to India from many European cities, but a stop is necessary for the 16–21 hour trips from New York or Los Angeles. The main internal or domestic airline is Indian Airlines, which flies between about 60 Indian cities and also serves neighboring countries. Another airline, Vayudoot, flying smaller aircraft than Indian Airlines, connects other cities.

India operates more than 400 merchant ships, most of which are ocean-going, with the remainder used for coastal trade. There are ten major ports, of which Calcutta and Vishakhapatanam on the east coast and Bombay and Cochin on the west coast are the biggest. New ports are being created at Tuticorin on the east coast near India's southernmost tip, Cape Cormorin, and at Mangalore on the west coast.

Telephones and space age communication

India has put satellites into space with the help of Soviet rockets, and has had limited success at launching its own rockets. The government wants to use satellites to improve communications between cities and the rural areas, as well as for such things as weather forecasting. Satellite broadcasting is the only way the government can hope to reach all the people with television. Television broadcasting by satellite is already in use, and has helped to bring basic education to the villages for such things as literacy and health campaigns. However, the cost of providing televisions and the decoders necessary to receive the satellite signals for all Indian villages would be enormous. It is likely to be a long time before television rivals the enormous popularity of movies in rural India.

Cochin, on the coast of the far southwest, is one of India's major ports, moving over 4.9 million tons of goods a year. There is also a thriving shipyard that builds huge bulk tankers.

Some people feel that the government is perhaps being too ambitious with its space age plans and that it ought to concentrate on improving the existing telephone system, which is not very good. It is quite easy to make international telephone calls from Bombay, Madras, or Delhi. However, Calcutta has a telephone system that suffers badly when the rains come, and telephoning the smaller cities from the major ones is not easy.

A free press
The right of free speech, that is, the right of anyone to express his or her views, is regarded as very important in India. As a result, a lively press exists, and newspapers and magazines comment on all aspects of government and politics and are not afraid to criticize the actions of the government. When Indira Gandhi introduced censorship and started arresting journalists during the state of emergency in the mid-1970s, it proved to be a very unpopular measure and eventually led to her defeat in the next elections. Today, around 800 daily newspapers are published in India in many languages, and the newspapers have again become important in allowing the people to have free speech. The independent press provides a balance to the radio and television services, which are under government control.

10   Health and Education

Levels of health and hygiene are slowly getting better in India, thanks to improvements in water supply and increases in the numbers of doctors and other medical workers, and of hospitals and clinics. The government has committed large amounts of money to expanding the areas of the country where western-style medicine is available, and to controlling the spread of infectious diseases by vaccination campaigns. India also has traditional health care, known as *ayurvedic* medicine, which uses herbs and spices rather than drugs for treatment. Hinduism encourages yoga as a way of relaxing both body and mind, and most Indian religions stress the importance of meditation for a healthy life.

Traditional medicines emphasizing herbs and oils are widely used. This form of medicine is called ayurveda, *meaning "knowledge of life." There are over 300,000 ayurvedic medicine men.*

Successes and problems in health care

India has achieved particular success in recent years in controlling the spread of diseases. Smallpox has been eliminated completely, and malaria is less common as a result of a national campaign to spray homes and stagnant water to control the mosquito population, since these insects carry the disease. Many homes now have the symbol of the National Malaria Eradication Program painted on them showing the date of the last spraying. Deaths from smallpox, plague, and famine are things of the past.

Another big improvement is the reduction in deaths of babies, although around a million children a year still die before they reach their first birthday. These deaths are partly a result of disease, stemming from poor hygiene and living conditions, and partly due to lack of food or poor-quality food. Though India produces enough food to feed everyone, some people are too poor to afford to buy food. Hygiene is a major problem, too. Outside the cities, very few homes have a toilet or running water. The normal practice is for people to use the fields as toilets. The water supply usually comes from wells and rivers in or near the fields, so the chances of drinking water that has become contaminated by sewage are very great. The crowded conditions of urban shanty towns also lead to unhygienic conditions. The fatal disease, cholera, which results from contaminated water, can very easily grow to epidemic proportions when it breaks out in a densely populated area.

One of the greatest health problems still facing India is leprosy. Leprosy is a virus disease spread

Health centers have been established all over India in an attempt to control some of the diseases like malaria, tuberculosis, and leprosy, which are widespread. There is only one doctor for every 4,200 people, so the task is difficult.

by close contact, and it eventually leads to the wasting away of limbs, causing bad deformity. As many as four million Indians suffer from leprosy, and in around a million cases the disease has led to deformity. If treated in time, this disease is now easily cured, but India still has a long way to go to bring leprosy completely under control. People suffering from leprosy generally take to the streets and beg. Fortunately both Hinduism and Islam encourage the giving of gifts and money to poor and disabled people.

Sixty years ago, the average Indian's life expectancy at birth was 26 years. In other words, the chances of a baby surviving to adulthood were not very great. Today, life expectancy in India is around 56. This improvement in life expectancy is obviously a sign of much-improved health care, but the fact that people are living longer puts an additional strain on the country's ability to cope with an expanding population.

Family planning

For more than 30 years India has encouraged birth control, or family planning, to try to reduce the rate at which the country's population is increasing. Posters can be seen everywhere encouraging people to limit the size of their families, saying for example, "Two's enough." People in the cities are more likely than rural people to understand that they can devote more love, care, and money to a smaller family than if they have large numbers of children. In rural areas, the knowledge that many children die when they are still young makes parents more inclined to have large families to ensure that some children survive. If several children survive, they argue, then there are more people to help work in the fields or to look after the parents in their old age. There is also the problem that in rural areas fewer people can read and fewer people have televisions. This makes it more difficult to explain to parents the advantages and techniques of limiting family size than it is in the cities, where the message can be communicated through poster and television advertising.

Education

Only about 36 percent of India's large population can read and write, and many more women than men are unable to read, or are illiterate. Illiteracy is the biggest obstacle to the spread of

understanding about health, hygiene, and family planning. The cycle of poverty and lack of education is difficult to break. The poor cannot afford to feed their children or send them to school, so often they do not learn about ways of improving their lives.

Schools are widely available in India. Up to the age of 14, education is free and all children are supposed to attend. However, this does not mean that all children go to school, since parents may expect the children to work in the fields to increase the family's earnings. Education is the responsibility of the state rather than central government, and this means that the spread of education and literacy varies widely. The government wants to encourage people to be able to read and write in more than one language, but recognizes that raising the level of literacy in one language is the most urgent priority.

Secondary and higher level education is also widely available in India. Unlike primary education, though, higher level and college education are not free. Family poverty restricts the numbers of pupils taking advantage of what is available. Indian higher education is on a par with the best in the world, especially in producing technically trained people. This has helped India to develop high-tech industry. However, many Indians go abroad for higher education, and some of them never return to their own country because they find that the opportunities for finding good jobs suited to their particular skills are better overseas.

These Sikh girls are studying at the University of Lucknow. Until recently education was not considered important for women, but now there are a million female students and 2.5 million male students at India's 125 universities.

11 India Today

One of India's greatest problems is the ever-growing population. Old Delhi is the most densely populated of India's cities. However, it is typical of the other cities in that a lot of the buildings are old and run down. There are also many very poor people, most of whom have come from the country looking for work. These people are often homeless and sleep in the streets.

When Rajiv Gandhi became prime minister in 1984, he promised to prepare India for the twenty-first century. In other words, he was no longer content to see India accept second best in terms of its industrial output. He found that promise easier to make than to put into effect. For while India has the resources to make it an industrial nation, such as minerals, energy, skills, and cheap manpower, it also has the major problem of the poverty of the vast majority of its people to overcome. If the government spends more money on industry at the expense of agriculture, it risks widening the already wide

gap between India's rich and its poor. Reducing poverty is undoubtedly India's greatest challenge, despite the considerable advances that have been made in recent years.

The Punjab problem

India also has political problems; the most serious is the one facing Punjab state. A number of Sikhs in India's richest state want to break away and become an independent nation, which they call Khalistan, or "the land of the pure." Unfortunately, they have been pursuing their cause with a campaign of killings that has left thousands dead in the last few years. The government's response, and in particular Mrs. Gandhi's order in 1984 for the army to enter the Sikh's holiest shrine, the Golden Temple in Amristar, has deepened the sense of separateness that many Sikhs feel. The government has to try hard not to upset particular language or religious groups when there is neither a common language nor a common religion to bind Indians together. The government also worries that events in Punjab might give rise to other breakaway movements elsewhere. For example, the Nepali-speaking people of the area around Darjeeling in West Bengal have called for a homeland of their own, to be called Gorkhaland. The Bodo tribe of Assam have also been campaigning for a state of their own.

A regional power

Rajiv Gandhi's plan to take a strong, industrially developed India into the twenty-first century also had another side to it. He wanted India to be a

Indian prime minister, Rajiv Gandhi (center, first row) attended the Non-aligned Summit Conference held in 1986 at Harare, Zimbabwe. India was one of the founder members of the Non-aligned Movement and has largely followed a course of non-alignment with any other country since independence.

strong military and diplomatic power, a regional superpower. The war between India and Pakistan in 1971, which led to the former East Pakistan becoming the independent nation of Bangladesh, demonstrated India's military strength. Three years later, in 1974, India exploded a nuclear device in the desert of the state of Rajasthan. The government does not admit to having nuclear weapons, but it certainly has nuclear power for nonmilitary purposes, and is developing nuclear-powered naval vessels. Even if it is not already a nuclear power, it could swiftly become one.

India also plays an active role in international diplomacy. It has been a member of the British Commonwealth since it became independent, and has voiced its strong views over the treatment of nonwhite people in South Africa, where many people of Indian origin are settled. India was also a founding member of the Non-aligned Movement, a group of countries who wish to remain separate from the influences of either the United States or the Soviet Union. In fact, over the past 20 years, India has been a close friend of the Soviet Union, but that friendship stops short of any military arrangements. Most recently India became a member of the South Asian Association for Regional Cooperation, which groups together seven South Asian nations. India is easily the biggest and strongest member. The Association aims to overcome some of the suspicion that exists between the neighbors, notably between India and Pakistan, by encouraging greater trade and cooperation.

The food cycle
India has reached the all-important goal of producing enough food to feed all its people. The challenge now is to improve the quantity and quality of food eaten by the poorest people and to try to eliminate malnutrition. However, as India still has a growing population, it needs to continue to increase the amount of food produced. To do this India needs to improve the yield of cereals and grains from the land, and to increase the amount of land that benefits from additional water supplies or irrigation. The planners also need to work on ways of coping with the floods resulting from the monsoons in order to avoid crop loss, and to make use of the excess waters for irrigation. For centuries India has been totally dependent on the monsoons to

The northern plains of Ladakh in Jammur and Kashmir are now covered with abundant wheat. This is evidence of the "Green Revolution" in northwestern India.

provide water for both people and crops. It is not possible to change the seasons or when and how much rain comes. However, by improved water management on the ground, India can hope to reduce dependence on the monsoons and increase crop yields.

Conclusion

India does not expect to tackle all of its problems at once. It is, after all, one of the world's oldest civilizations, and history shows that it has already enjoyed several high points of civilization. This century it has suffered economically, and the country is having to deal with the problems associated with poverty at the same time as it experiences the benefits of industrialization. Perhaps before the twenty-first century, India will have broken out of the poverty trap and become once again a great and prosperous nation. For the present, it does at least have a degree of stability and a democratic system of government that are the envy of many other nations.

Index

© Heinemann Children's Reference 1990
This edition originally published 1990 by Heinemann Children's Reference, a division of Heinemann Educational Books, Ltd.